CW00970884

Other Titles by Dr. Javad Nurbakhsh

Divani Nurbakhsh
The Truths of Love
In the Tavern of Ruin
In the Paradise of the Sufis
Spiritual Poverty in Sufism
Jesus in the Eyes of the Sufis
Sufi Symbolism
The Psychology of Sufism
Masters of the Path
Traditions of the Prophet
Sufi Women
The Great Satan 'Eblis'
Dogs from a Sufi Point of View
Sufism

DISCOURSES ON THE SUFI PATH

Copyright © 1996 by Dr. Javad Nurbakhsh

All rights reserved under International and Pan-American Copyright Conventions. No part of this book may be used or reproduced in any manner whatsoever without written permission except in the case of brief quotations embodied in critical articles and reviews.

Published by Khaniqahi Nimatullahi Publications
U.K.: 41 Chepstow Place, London W2 4TS
U.S.A.: 306 West 11th Street, New York, N.Y. 10014

Library of Congress Cataloging-in-Publication Data

Nūrbakhsh, Javād
[Chihil kalām va sī payām. English]
Discourses on the Sufi path/Javad Nurbakhsh
p. cm.
ISBN 0-933546-58-0 (hb: alk. paper)
1. Sufism—Prayer books and devotions. I. Title.

BP189.62.N8613 1996 96-8009
297'.4—dc20 CIP

Printed in the United States of America

DR. JAVAD NURBAKHSH

Translated by Alireza Nurbakhsh

DISCOURSES ON THE SUFI PATH

KHANIQAHI NIMATULLAHI PUBLICATIONS
LONDON NEW YORK

In the Name of the Bestower of Light

This book was composed in
heartfelt moments. My hope
is that it will address the
questions of those seekers
who are receptive and open
to the states of the heart.

CONTENTS

DISCOURSES

CHIVALRY 13

FESTIVAL 15

NAMAZ AND FASTING 17

TRAVELING AND SOCIAL CONDUCT 19

LOVE 21

PILGRIMAGE 23

PAIN AND CURE 25

THE TWO PRINCIPAL MESSAGES OF SUFISM 27

SINCERITY 28

THE DROP AND THE OCEAN 30

GOD 32

ABSENCE AND PRESENCE 35

THE PATH 37

ONE WHO KNOWS ONE'S LORD KNOWS ONE'S SELF . 39

LOVE AND REASON 41

CONSTANCY 43

ATTRACTION AND SOCIAL CONDUCT 45

A SELFLESS MASTER 47

SUBMISSION 49

ETIQUETTE AND ETHICS 51

SIN AND MERIT 53

DETACHMENT FROM THE WORLD 55
THE MEANING OF *"YA 'ALI!"* 57
UNBELIEF 58
THE PRISONERS OF THE *NAFS* 60
QUESTIONING 63
MASTER AND DISCIPLE 66
RIGHT AND WRONG 69
SPIRITUAL COMBAT 71
THE FAMILY 72
KHANIQAH AND RELIGIOUS ASSEMBLIES 74
GOD'S BENEVOLENCE AND WRATH 75
SELFLESSNESS 77
BREATH IS THE TRUTH 78
FREEWILL AND DETERMINISM 80
WHO IS A SUFI? 81
THE INTELLECT 83
THE BENEFITS OF GOING TO THE *KHANIQAH* 84
DEVOTION 86
RULES AND MANNERS 87

APHORISMS 89

DISCOURSES

CHIVALRY

Before Islam appeared, the tradition of chivalry *(javanmardi)* in the Middle East was maintained through the training of men to be chevaliers *(javanmardan)*.

The tradition of chivalry involved consideration for others *(morowwat)*, self-sacrifice *(ithar)*, devotion *(fada-kari)*, the helping of the unfortunate and unprotected, kindness towards all created beings, keeping one's word and self-effacement—all qualities that were later to emerge as the noble attributes of the perfect human being from the point of view of Sufism.

In addition to these attributes of a true human being, the chevaliers were committed to a particular code of etiquette and conventions, from which the main objective and principles of chivalry or *javanmardi* were derived.

With the appearance of Islam, these chevaliers embraced the religion of Islam while retaining the conventions of chivalry, thereby founding the creed of Sufism on the basis of both Islam and chivalry. Thus, the etiquette of the chevaliers became part of the practice of the *khaniqah* and of the Sufis.

Gradually, as the philosophy of the Unity of Being *(wahdato'l-wojud)* and divine love were made more profound and appealing by Sufi masters, the tradition of chivalry, hand-in-hand with it, gained an extraordinary influence and currency. The spirit of Sufism consisted of focusing one's gaze in one direction (towards God) through the power of love, and its method was to cultivate a humane code of ethics, which was equated with that of the chevaliers.

Sufism, then, has both an outward and an inward aspect:

Its inward aspect consists of traveling the Path and traversing its stations to attain the level of subsistence-through-God *(baqa')*. Its outward aspect consists of the tradition of chivalry, which constitutes the development of the attributes of perfect human beings.

Sufis must know that they are the standard-bearers of the school of humanity and of the tradition of chivalry in the world today, and they must not allow modern civilization to destroy noble human qualities—a civilization which, from the outward point of view, raises human beings to the greatest heights, while at the same time lowering their inward qualities to a level beneath that of animals.

In the materialistic civilization of today, Sufis must strive to be examples of noble human beings in order to draw the desires and inclinations of others towards these humane attributes—attributes that are unique to the human species.

Sufis must exhibit to humanity the effects and results of the spiritual paradise they have discovered on the Sufi Path, so that others may be aware that their material paradise is worthless in comparison.

FESTIVAL

The Sufis have two festivals: the ordinary and the elect. The ordinary festival for all Sufis is described by Sana'i in the following verse:

The Sufis celebrate two festivals each breath;
Spiders celebrate by making feasts of flies.

The meaning of Sana'i's verse is that while the fundamentalist clergy are like spiders who seek at every moment, with the breath of their preaching, to entangle ordinary people in their webs, Sufis observe two festivals with every breath. When Sufis breathe in, they concentrate on God's Attributes, and when they breathe out, they take refuge in God's Essence. This represents the return of the heart to its origin, the Beloved, at every moment, with every breath. The practice of loving through remembrance of the Beloved is like a festival, inspiring joy in the Sufi. According to the Koran: "Indeed, we are God's, and indeed, to Him we are returning." (II: 156)

The elect festival is sought by all Sufis, although only a few achieve it. This festival is described by Majzub Tabrizi in the following verse:

For Your Majzub, *attracted only to You,*
New Year's Eve is no festival.
He will celebrate a festival
only on the day he beholds Your Face.

The elect festival of the Sufis is celebrated when one is severed from the creation *(khalq)* and joined with the Real *(haqq).* It takes place on the day of union with the Absolute Beloved which is the Sufi's lifelong desire, the prospect of which elates the Sufi's heart. This is the day when the drop settles on the vast surface of the Ocean and views the Ocean with the eyes of the Ocean.

It is this encounter to which the Koran refers in the passage: "Whoever hopes for the encounter with his Lord, let him act with righteous actions and ascribe no partners in the worship of his Lord" (XVIII: 110). 'Righteous action' refers to acting with no thought of merit or reward. Ansari comments on this passage as follows: "All creation loves life, and death is hard for all created beings; the Sufi, however, hastens towards death in the hope of finally encountering God and beholding His Face."

NAMAZ AND FASTING

A Bedouin was once walking with his dog in the desert, carrying a skin of water on his shoulders, crying pitifully as he went along. When asked by someone why he was crying, he replied, "Because my dog is dying of thirst."

"Why don't you give him some of your water, then?" the questioner asked.

"Because I might need the water myself."

In the same way, most *darvishes* are ready to listen to talk about Sufism, but they are reluctant to put it into practice. They enjoy reading Sufi books and hearing talks about Sufism, but when it comes time to do something about it, they have second thoughts. I talk about this now in the hope that you may become aware of what you are doing—although I know how difficult this is.

It is said that the disciples of Hasan Basri appealed to their master, saying, "O master, our hearts are asleep, for your words have no effect on us. What can we do?" Hasan replied, "If only you were merely asleep, because shaking can awaken a sleeper! But your hearts are dead, for however much I shake them, they do not wake up!"

I have decided to say a few words about daily prayers *(namaz)* and fasting because the creed of love has its own special *namaz* and fasting, in addition to the conventional ones. These are based on a particular etiquette *(adab)* and set of conventions, of which I shall give a concise account so that you may have a better idea of the requirements of the Path you claim to follow.

The Sufi *namaz* is only two *rak'at*-s. In order to perform these two *rak'at*-s, Sufis do their ablution *(wozu)* with the water of love, then face the *qebla* of "And wherever you turn, there is God's countenance"

(II: 115), and repeat *'Allaho akbar'* four times.

With the first *'Allaho akbar',* they put the world and all its inhabitants behind them.

With the second *'Allaho akbar',* they forget the hereafter.

With the third *'Allaho akbar',* they cast the very thought of anything other than God out of their hearts.

With the fourth *'Allaho akbar',* they forget even themselves.

Only then do they begin the prayer, performing the two *rak'at*-s sincerely over the corpse of their ego *(nafs).* Once they have properly completed this prayer, they become joined with God.

Nowadays, the ablution for this *namaz* takes most Sufis years and years. If they manage to complete the ablution, they have to spend a long time on the first *'Allaho akbar',* and there are very few who get to the second one and forget the two worlds.

As for the Sufi fast, it is not simply a matter of fasting one month a year. The Sufi fasts every day from loving what is other than God; yet even a single day of such a manly fast is beyond the capacity of most people!

So, for those of you who can do neither the Sufi prayers nor the Sufi fast, how do you expect to be offered the stations of Hallaj and Bayazid? As Rumi expresses it:

> *Like children who turn their skirts*
> *into make-believe horses,*
> *You ride your skirts and aspire*
> *to the battlefield!*

TRAVELING AND SOCIAL CONDUCT

The expression *'sair-o soluk'* is employed quite often in Persian, both in speech and in writing. Few, however, have understood its true meaning in Sufism.

Literally, the term *'sair-o soluk'* is composed of two words where each word can be explained separately in the following manner: First, *'sair'* (traveling) signifies the purification of the Sufi's inward being on the Path towards spiritual perfection. It refers to the Sufi's relationship with God, to the Sufi's struggle to be ever more conscious of God through constant remembrance of Him and to forget himself, so as to advance farther and farther along the Path. This is an inward matter, particular to the individual.

On the other hand, *'soluk'* (social conduct) refers to a fundamental principle relating to the society of Sufis as a community. That is, *soluk* pertains to how Sufis should conduct themselves with respect to society as a whole. This is a vitally important aspect of Sufism, and it is imperative for Sufis to pay attention to it. In general, someone who is identified as a Sufi from the point of view of society must act as a model human being, and if such a person, who others associate with Sufism, behaves improperly in relationships with others or does things that are contrary to human considerations, that person does harm to the school of Sufism and to Sufis as a whole.

In order to instruct and correct their disciples, Sufi masters in the past have resorted to various tales and anecdotes, sometimes using animals to illustrate their points. As an example, it is related that Abu Sa'id 'Abo'l-Khayr was walking down the street one day with a group of disciples when a dog bit at the garment of one of the *darvishes*. The *darvish* raised his walking stick and hit the dog. The dog then went to the master, Abu Sa'id, complaining about his treatment at the hands of the *darvish*, that it should be beaten for having bitten at his clothes. The master, Abu Sa'id, replied, "Why don't you bite me in return?" The dog protested, "But I am complaining about something else! I don't want revenge. He was dressed as a Sufi and hence deceived me. I assumed that since he was a Sufi, I could bite him freely without him hurting me!"

This story illustrates the importance of Sufi conduct and indicates that *sair* and *soluk*, although considered separate aspects of Sufism, are in fact complementary. That is, one who does not observe the conduct of a Sufi has not attained perfection in the work of spiritual traveling, while, at the same time, one who has advanced spiritually has the conduct towards others of a perfected human being. As a result, masters of the Path are able to identify the progress of Sufis in reaching more advanced spiritual stations and the extent of their traveling towards God by means of their conduct.

Fundamentally, then, traveling and social conduct are a pair of wings with which a human being takes flight towards perfection, for no one can fly with only one wing!

LOVE

All human beings during their lives experience love and friendship to some extent. Human love can be classified into three basic categories according to its intensity, quality and limitations.

The first form of love is friendship based on social conventions where two people behave in accordance with the principle: "I for myself, you for yourself; we love each other, but we have no expectations of each other." This form of love is that of ordinary people, whose love relationships tend to be of this nature.

The second form of love is based on a more solid foundation, and those who live together usually experience this kind of love: "I for you, you for me; we love each other, having mutual expectations of each other." This form of love includes profound love as well as the love found within most families, involving emotional give and take on a more or less equal footing.

The third kind of love transcends all conventions based on mutual expectations, being founded on the following principle: "I am for you, you are for whoever you choose; I accept whatever you want without any expectations whatsoever."

The Sufi's devotion to God and to the master of the Path exemplifies this latter form of love. This third kind of love is not based upon any constraints or conditions; the Sufi who possesses this kind of love says with contentment and submission to God: "I am satisfied with whatever You want, without any expectations, and love You without any thought of reward."

The Sufi's love of God involves no expectation of reward or fear of punishment, for the Sufi does not have any wishes and demands. The Sufi embraces and loves God's wrath as much as His grace, His hardheartedness as much as His fidelity.

Only a few Sufis have managed to annihilate themselves in the Beloved through the path of such love and friendship. It is about these Sufis that Rumi has said:

Everything is the Beloved,
and the lover but a veil;
The Beloved is alive,
while the lover is dead.

Thus, we see that the highest form of human love is 'Sufi love'. Alas, it is a polo ball that only the most distinguished and perfected of humans are worthy of putting into play.

PILGRIMAGE

Pilgrimage *(hajj)* requires intention, and the goal is to reach the lane of the Beloved. There are two kinds of pilgrimage: the ordinary and the elect.

The ordinary pilgrimage is the journey to the Ka'ba, while the elect pilgrimage is the journey towards its Owner. The ordinary pilgrimage is to circle the four physical walls of that house, while the elect pilgrimage is to visit the Ka'ba of the heart.

The ordinary pilgrimage is to travel to Mecca and arrive at the Ka'ba, while the elect pilgrimage is to leave existence behind and arrive at the valley of annihilation.

The ordinary pilgrimage is to carry out what the Lord has commanded, while the elect pilgrimage is to yearn to behold the Beloved.

The ordinary pilgrimage is to hope for the reward of attaining paradise, while the elect pilgrimage is to behold the compassionate Beloved and attain unity.

The ordinary pilgrimage is to perform one's duties where observance of etiquette is the primary principle, while the elect pilgrimage is to separate from all others at the station of union with the Beloved.

The ordinary pilgrimage requires physical maturity, mental stability, outward freedom and financial ability, while the fundamental conditions of the elect pilgrimage are spiritual attainment, freedom from the prison of the *nafs*, patience, the zeal of love and the capacity to see the Beloved.

When the ordinary resolve to make the pilgrimage to the Ka'ba, they set out by whatever means they have at their disposal to reach Mecca, put on the pilgrimage garment and circle the Ka'ba, whereas when the elect yearn to behold the Owner of the Ka'ba, they turn the heart's blood into their provision for the Way, ride on the horse of love, drunkenly tear off the flimsy garments of transitory ego-consciousness, don the garment of nonexistence and circle the Ka'ba of the heart, thereby discovering its Owner.

The purified Sufis belong to the category of the elect. While yearning to behold the Beloved, they circle the Ka'ba of the heart, consigning self and all personal expectations to oblivion at the station of union, and become purified by the light of divine unity *(tawhid)* in the circle of Oneness.

PAIN AND CURE

In Sufi literature, many words have been devoted to describing spiritual states, one of which is 'pain', a word that has been given various meanings.

First of all, it must be made clear that 'pain' is a psychological force existing within the Sufi. This force guides the Sufi to perfection and to the perception of Reality. This is the meaning of the term when used to describe various states in such expressions as the 'pain of seeking', the 'pain of love' and the 'pain of God'.

Another meaning of pain refers to the pain of 'separation from the Beloved', where the one in pain, in separation, seeks union and cure. As Baba Taher expresses it:

One person is content with pain, another with cure;
One is content with union, another with separation.
I am content with whatever the Beloved desires,
Be it cure or pain, union or separation.

True lovers prefer the Beloved's desires to their own, being content with whatever the Beloved desires—"be it cure or pain, union or separation."

Another meaning of pain, the one closest to its common usage, refers to a state causing sadness and suffering. This kind of pain is not present in pure Sufis, for they have no desires and are content with whatever contents God. Thus, the Sufi is always joyful; the one who is truly a Sufi has no reason to be sad. Anyone who is sad and behaves as if he is suffering has not comprehended the true meaning of Sufism, which is surrender to God.

In the words of Hafez:

If there is any profit in this marketplace,
it is with the contented Sufi.
O Lord, grant me the blessing
of Sufism and contentment!

Finally, 'pain' has also been employed in yet another context, that of the 'pain without cure', an expression certain Sufis have taken to mean love. As Rumi says:

O love, you're known to everyone
under a different name;
Last night I gave you another name,
that of the 'pain without cure'.

In our view, love cannot be said to mean pain without cure, for the love-crazed heart becomes linked to the spirit of unity by the grace of love, which is the commander of the forces of the realm of unity. Hence, insofar as love distances the Sufi from multiplicity and created beings, it constitutes pain for him, while at the same time, by conveying the Sufi to unity and God, it becomes a cure. Thus, love is both pain and cure.

THE TWO PRINCIPAL MESSAGES OF SUFISM

The school of Sufism has two principal messages, and whatever has been said concerning the rules and manners of Sufism is secondary when compared to these two.

The first message is psychological and heart-related: that Sufis must confirm, seek and see only the Absolute Being and not think about anything else.

The second, which is derived from the first, is social and ethical: that Sufis must exemplify the highest humanitarian and ethical values.

In the first place, these messages instruct people to be noble human beings and to respect, love and serve God's creation. Second, by focusing on the existence of the unity of all creation, these messages instill in people the method of looking solely in one direction and seeing everything as One. Thus, Sufism is a school of unity and ethical purification which, regardless of race and culture, can be applied to all human beings equally.

It should be noted, however, that merely by registering in the school of Sufism and participating in the Sufis' gatherings, a person does not become a Sufi. Rather, one has to strive to succeed in the practice of Sufism, namely, to be purified in such a way that one's outward behavior is decorated by humane values and one's inner being is ornamented by divine attributes.

Thus, if you encounter a human being who claims to be a Sufi and behaves contrary to the human code of ethics, do not ask, "What kind of Sufi is this?" Rather, it would be better to ask, "What kind of person would this have been had he not been a Sufi?"

SINCERITY

The capital of the Path is, in truth, nothing other than sincerity. Sincerity has been defined as 'showing yourself as you really are' and 'being inwardly what you show yourself to be'.

One may speak of three stages of sincerity: sincerity with oneself, sincerity with the master, and sincerity with God.

1. Sincerity with oneself

If we say that Sufism means 'attaining unity', then 'sincerity with oneself' signifies 'unifying one's outward being with one's inward being' and thereby establishing unity in oneself.

If there is no unity of the outward with the inward, there can be no unity of character. This disharmony between one's outward and inward being generates anxiety and depression. Only through the power of sincerity can one bring about psychophysical unity in oneself, can one enjoy psychological health.

Hence, the results of 'sincerity with oneself' are liberation from the anxiety that stems from disharmony of character and the establishment of psychological health.

2. Sincerity with the master

At this stage of sincerity, through the attraction of the sincerity and love of the master, the Sufi in whom psychophysical unity has been established, becomes unified with the master. This is known on the Path as 'annihilation in the master' which in itself, is a form of 'identification', a term current in contemporary psychology: In this case, the Sufis call it 'transcendental identification'. At this stage, the Sufi's ego, or self-identity, is annihilated in the master, and the Sufi totally forgets himself. An example of this form of unity was the annihilation of Rumi's ego in his master, Shams-e Tabrizi.

This sincerity frees the Sufi from the anxieties of life and the anxiety that arises from fear of dying and being obliterated, such that he feels as Rumi did when he exclaimed:

I was dead; I have come alive!
I was weeping; now I am laughing!
The fortune of love has arrived,
and I have become everlasting fortune!

Most Sufi masters equate annihilation in the master with annihilation in God.

3. Sincerity with God

Sincerity with God is the highest level of sincerity. At this stage of sincerity, which is the result of 'sincerity with oneself' and 'sincerity with the master', unity between the Sufi and God becomes established through the power of sincerity and gnosis. This is known as 'annihilation in God', which refers to the identification of the part with the Whole.

At this stage, the Sufi loses his ego, or self-identity, and becomes the Whole, brought into eternal life, for the Truth exists forever.

THE DROP AND THE OCEAN

If we liken God to the ocean and the human individual to a drop, we can say that the function of Sufism is to carry the drop to the ocean.

A master of the Path is like a river linked to the ocean. The drop must commit itself to the river so that it can be carried to the ocean.

Needless to say, for the drop to reach the ocean with the help of the river, it must first meet many challenges. It must put up with a great deal of turbulence arising from its various encounters in the river so that it may eventually merge with the ocean in serenity and stability.

In certain circumstances, it is possible for the drop to merge directly with the ocean, a process referred to as 'attraction'. In this case, however, the drop does not have the advantage of being able to guide others, because it has not itself traveled the path of the river.

Given that the river and the ocean are fundamentally one, annihilation in a master is considered to be the same as annihilation in God. Submission to a master means that the master blinds the self-seeing eyes—or the 'drop-consciousness'—of the disciple, and brings sight to one's God-seeing eyes, or 'ocean-consciousness'.

Only when the drop has submitted to the river, and ultimately the ocean, can it forget its 'drop-ness'. When the drop finally merges with the ocean, it sees through the eyes of the ocean that it *is* the ocean.

The drop, of course, must be in contact with the river and the ocean in order to be absorbed in them. The remembrance *(zekr)* given by a master to the Sufi is the only means of bringing him into such contact that he may be snatched up by their attraction. If the drop merely settles on the bank of the river or the shore of the ocean, it will lose nothing of its 'drop-ness'. It must throw itself into the water if it wishes to give up its self-existence. This is why Sufism is said to entail becoming, and not simply hearing or reading.

GOD

From the Sufi's point of view, God is Absolute Being, and whatever exists is a determination or manifestation of Him. The Sufis maintain that all being exists through God's Being without which there would be nothing. As Rumi says:

We are nonexistence, displaying the illusion of existence;
You are Absolute Being and our only true existence.

In the words of the Koran: "All things are perishing but His Face" (XXVIII: 88), with the understanding that there is nothing but Him in the abode of existence.

The Sufis do not separate the realm of existence from God's existence. The Koranic verse, "God is the Light of the heavens and the earth" (XXIV: 35), has been interpreted by the traditional Islamic clergy to mean that God is the source of all illumination for the heavens and the earth. The Sufis, on the other hand, take this to mean that God is the very being, the reality of the heavens and the earth.

The insight that there is only one Absolute Being in the whole universe, and that whatever exists does so through His existence, has been called the philosophy of the "Unity of Being" *(wahdato'l-wojud).*

To be more precise, however, this is not a philosophy at all. A philosophy is something invented by the mind and hence subject to change. The awareness of the Unity of Being, though, is a perception of the heart and consequently everlasting and unchanging. Philosophy pertains to the mind and discourse, whereas perception of the Unity of Being pertains to love, revelation and vision. Therefore, in our view, it is better to use the term 'the principle', rather than the philosophy, of the Unity of Being.

To illustrate what is meant by the principle of the 'Unity of Being', the Sufis have used many analogies. Three of them are particularly apt:

To begin with, if we liken Absolute Being to an ocean, then the waves of this ocean can be thought of as individual beings, the true reality of which is the water. The transitory form of each being is the individual wave, which lasts for but a moment and is then obliterated, whereas the reality of the wave—that is, the water—is everlasting. Until one becomes aware of one's wave form, one can know nothing of the water. When the concept of the ocean as transitory waves disappears, one will then realize that there is in reality nothing but the water. Hence, the great Sufis have annihilated their wave-selves in the water of Absolute Being, crying from the depths of their souls expressions like "I am the Truth," "Glory be to My sublime station," and "There is nothing under this garment but God," expressions that leave people of the world astounded and amazed. In the words of Shah Nimatullah:

Wave, sea, and bubble—
all three are one;
Though there may appear to be many and few,
in truth there is but One.

In another analogy, Absolute Being has been compared to light and individual beings to shadows. As long as the shadow remains a shadow, it can know nothing of the light.

If the light moves away from the shadow, the shadow will always follow it. Thus, if one attempts to pursue the Truth under one's own power—that is, as a shadow—one will never attain it. Such an action in fact indicates that the Truth is actually moving away from one. Only when the light moves toward the shadow, thereby relieving it of its 'shadow-ness', will the shadow become the light.

As Maghrebi has said:

No one can journey towards God on his own feet;
To arrive at God's district, one must go with God's feet.

In the third and final analogy, Absolute Being is conceived as a point, and individual beings as lines or patterns, springing into existence from this single point. Whatever form is displayed outwardly is, in reality, merely transitory. Whatever form we see is in truth no more than a point. In the *Golshan-e raz,* Shabestari has written:

All these forms of 'otherness'
are in reality but illusions from you.
What makes the point appear a circle
is but the speed with which it moves.

As it says in the Koran, "Everything passes away; what remains is only the Face of your Lord, He of Majesty and Honor" (LV: 26-7).

Thus, according to the Sufi's point of view, the realm of individual existence, which is one of the levels of being, is imaginary from the perspective of 'shadowness', while it is nothing but Being from the perspective of Reality. In the words of Shah Nimatullah:

Throughout the world
and everything within it,
Whatever is seen is but a reflection of a ray
from the Face of the Friend.

ABSENCE AND PRESENCE

In Sufi terminology, 'absence' refers to 'absence from self and the world', while 'presence' signifies 'presence with God'. Masters of the Path have considered absence and presence to be two separate stations, maintaining that absence is the result of presence and that until presence comes about, absence cannot take place.

Absence without presence is not the goal, for many a mentally sick person may be absent from himself and from the world but not be present with God.

In Sufism there are two kinds of presence: 'presence of breath' and 'presence of heart'.

One who has presence of breath remembers God with every breath, never forgetting Him. Presence of this kind causes absence from the world. Presence of breath occurs through the Sufi's own volition when fired by love for God. In this state, the rememberer and the Remembered are still distinct from each other. Presence of breath takes place at the spiritual level of *nafs* at a time when the commanding *nafs* has become transformed into the blaming *nafs* and the *nafs*-at-rest. At this level, presence of heart may also occur, although only in flashes or for brief moments.

Presence of heart comes about due to persistence in presence of breath. Although presence of breath is a necessary condition for presence of the heart, it is not a sufficient condition for it. For one to attain presence of heart, the favor and support of God is also necessary. For presence of heart to come about, the spirit must be drawn by love or divine attraction. The consequence of presence of heart is absence from self, and with the attainment of presence of heart rememberer and Remembered finally become one.

Presence of heart is exclusive to the spiritual level of the heart. At this level, presence of heart is permanent and undiminished.

I have become so lost
from myself in remembering You
That I ask for news of myself
from whomever I meet on my way.
—Anon.

THE PATH

The Sufi Path *(tariqat)* is the preparatory course for becoming a Sufi. Whoever becomes a 'Sufi' in name should not think that he has become one in fact.

The Sufi is someone who swims in the sea of unity. The Path is the means by which the Sufi travels from the self to the edge of this sea. At the beginning of the Path, the Sufi worships thousands of idols, and in this sense is a true polytheist. The master of the Path helps the Sufi to the edge of the sea, assisting him in demolishing these idols, and enabling him to become a true unitarian *(movahhed).* The remembrances, and the spiritual states and stations of the Path are all measures for breaking the Sufi's idols. Manifestations, revelations and visions are God's favor for cleansing these idols from the Sufi's heart. It is in this context that Shebli said, "Sufism is all idolatry," and Ravim declared, "The Sufi does not experience state or station, for he has passed beyond states and stations."

When, with God's favor and a master's help, the Sufi reaches the edge of the sea, the master of the Path, through the grace of his friendship with God, removes the garment of egocentricity from the Sufi's body, releasing him to enter the sea of God's Attributes and Essence. It is at this point that the Sufi is truly a Sufi, and here that Sufism truly begins: there is no longer disciple or master, way or wayfarer.

A so-called master who cannot guide a traveler to the edge of the sea of annihilation has no choice but to divert the disciple's attention from God to himself by the display of miraculous powers, the recitation of pointless incantations, the unauthorized prescription of *zekr*, or the exposition of nonsensical doctrines about the Sufi Path. He only increases the idols worshipped by the disciple, reinforcing the disciple's idolatry.

Once disciples have outwardly entered the circle of those who follow the Path, they must be aware that in order to attain the station of a true Sufi, they have a long way ahead of them and at every moment they are in danger of losing their way. Indeed, it is impossible to traverse this Path without God's grace and that of His friends.

Thus, one should not consider oneself a Sufi; rather, it would be better to say that one has merely registered for a preparatory course in Sufism, that one is undertaking a series of examinations, hoping that some day one will be worthy of becoming a Sufi. As Rumi puts it:

Said the speaker, "There is no darvish in the world,
And if there were, he would be nonexistent.

He exists by virtue of his essence remaining,
But his attributes have become annihilated
in those of God.

He is nonexistent like a candle's flame
in the presence of the sun,
Though in reality he exists in the truest sense.

The essence of the flame exists, such that
If cotton touches it, it would be burned by the fire.

But in form it does not exist, for it gives you no light:
The sun has annihilated its attributive form."

ONE WHO KNOWS ONE'S LORD KNOWS ONE'S SELF

There is a Prophetic Tradition in which the Prophet says, "One who knows one's self knows one's Lord." Various interpretations of this tradition are possible, depending on whether we interpret 'Lord' to mean the one who commands or to mean God.

If we mean the former, then the psychological interpretation of this tradition is as follows:

We know that each person's behavior is, by and large, motivated by unconscious or subconscious conditioning; in other words, one's behavior is influenced by one's preexisting psychological state. Hence, one can say that whoever knows one's self, meaning the character traits and behavioral characteristics that have been influenced by the personalities of one's father and mother, as well as one's childhood environment and training, knows one's lord, which is, in fact, one's psychological personality.

If we understand 'Lord' to mean God, however, then the literal interpretation of the Tradition would be that whoever knows one's self knows one's God. Yet, as philosophers and gnostics have pointed out, humankind is transitory and knowledge of one's transitory nature does not amount to knowledge of the Eternal. Furthermore, a transitory being can never come to know the Eternal.

Sufis, however, strive to throw away the garment of transitoriness by the aid of love and to annihilate themselves in God. In this way, through Him they come to know Him. Thus, in interpreting this tradition they say:

1. One who knows oneself in annihilation knows one's Lord in Subsistence.
2. One who knows oneself in nonexistence knows one's Lord in Existence.

3. One who knows oneself as non-being knows one's Lord as Absolute Being.
4. One who knows oneself as poor knows one's Lord as Rich.
5. One who knows oneself as nothing knows one's Lord as Everything.

However, becoming nothing is a difficult task indeed, for as long as any trace of your being remains, you have not lost yourself in your Lord, who is everything.

LOVE AND REASON

The way of Sufism involves the annihilation of existence and liberation from self-centeredness and the self.

Individual reason—the faculty that is employed by philosophers and scientists—does not accept this way because it is concerned with the interests of the ego, self-love being its cult and creed. Only through love's decree can one forget what is other than God and embrace the eternal Beloved.

Let us listen to the dialogue between reason and love:

Reason says, "I am the blade of argumentation."
Love replies, "I am the sword of annihilation."
Reason says, "I depend on reasons."
Love replies, "As long as you are tied to reasons, you remain pathetic."
Reason says, "You won't attain the goal without the aid of my staff."
Love replies, "Not until you are completely burned by my fire will you attain True Existence."
Reason says, "Watch out for yourself and listen to good sense."
Love replies, "Let your self go and lose the sense of your ego."
Reason says, "Everything for yourself."
Love replies, "Yourself and everything else for Him."
Finally, love declares, "Pledge your life in the Way of the Beloved."
Reason replies, "That's too risky; give up the whole enterprise!"

Reason functions as the human being's trap in his hunting in the material world and is the means of pursuing his pleasures. Love functions as God's lasso, used to draw one to the truths of the spiritual world and the source of unity.

Reason operates on the basis of knowledge, logic and rote learning, while love operates on the basis of insight, divine favor and feeling.

Reason tries to know the sea and the drop by distinguishing between them, while love draws the drop into the ocean.

Reason is the foundation of self-display and self-satisfaction, while love is the substance of self-sacrifice and neediness.

In short, reason is the trusted prime minister of the government of the ego, while love is the commander-in-chief of the forces of the spirit.

The government of reason is composed of the *nafs*, its traits, and the constructs of the intellect, whereas the army of love is made up of the traits of the spirit and divine discoveries. In certain people, it is possible for some of the soldiers of love to serve reason while believing in and adhering to the spirit.

In the arena of the heart, reason is an advisor committed to protecting the interests of the ego, whereas love is a firebrand of a commander, putting existence to the torch. It rides down on reason and its ministers, defeating them in battle and taking over the land of the heart.

Thereupon, love, the victorious commander, claps the ego in irons and makes reason its prisoner and obedient servant. It disarms reason's guards, depriving them of their weapons of self-centeredness and pride. It plunders their treasury of worldly desires. It strips the soldiers of the *nafs* of their flimsy garments and clothes them in the finely woven, lustrous garments of the qualities of the spirit, which are the traits of perfect human beings, thereby transforming the animal soul into the soul-at-peace. Finally, it establishes the utopia of unity, peace and purity in the realm of the heart.

The role of Sufism in this battle is to support the army of love, so that it can conquer the land of the heart and attain that utopia.

CONSTANCY

One must walk upon the Sufi Path with the feet of love. On this Path, 'constancy' or 'steadfastness' *(esteqamat)* provides the provisions needed to carry one forward.

As Rumi puts it:

He asked, "Where is the affliction?"
I replied, "In the lane of Your love."
He asked, "What is your state there?"
I replied, "That of constancy."

The term, 'constancy', is taken from the Koranic passage in which God tells His Prophet: "Be constant, as you are commanded" (XI: 112); that is to say, "Be steadfast in what I have told you to do."

In the words of Shabestari:

When he committed himself
to the Way of God, he was firm
In observing the injunction:
"Be constant, as you are commanded."

Constancy means to step out of yourself and stand firm in God. Only the chevaliers *(javanmardan)* and the advanced on the Path can practice constancy in the lane of love. Feeling hurt, making excuses, getting distracted, being irresponsible, questioning, testing the master, ignoring orders given on the Path, making claims, doing exercises or reciting litanies that are not authorized, all serve to block the development of constancy or steadfastness in the Sufi.

In maintaining constancy, there were great Sufi masters who did not even dare to appeal to God, mortifying their desires in the crucible of oblivion, to the point that they became oblivious of their very constancy.

Those who are 'constant' declare, "We want God alone. We are standing firm until we cease to exist and there is only He." They also say, "O Lord, we don't distinguish between Your afflictions and Your blessings. We want whatever You want."

Abu 'Ali Jauzjani said, "Practice constancy; don't go looking for miracles, for it's your *nafs* that wants miracles, while God wants constancy from you." Constancy means steadfastness, that is to say, 'not seeing anything other than God.' Stand firm, and do not waver on the Path. Stand firm, and do not take hard the pressures of the Path. Meet difficulties and afflictions with courage. Stand firm, and do not let the challenges of the Path depress you or turn you away from the Path. If someone treats you badly, apologize to him! If someone irritates you, be thankful! If affliction visits you, consider it a necessary cure!

Constancy or steadfastness in following the instructions of God and the master is the true secret of success for the wayfarer. Whoever knows this secret and acts upon it will succeed.

ATTRACTION AND SOCIAL CONDUCT

When Sufis speak of attraction, they mean the divine attraction and grace directed to the lover and seeker of God. It must be stressed here that such attraction cannot be bestowed upon a heedless person. The sincere Sufi who acquires such a blessing, in addition to his innate aptitude, must have struggled along the Path of God for a long time. As the poet says:

The state of attraction to the Friend appears suddenly,
But it descends only upon an aware heart.

One who is attracted to God does not know anyone or anything but God, and, in comparison to the intellectuals of the Path, only this kind of person is worthy of being called 'the fool of God'.

Those who have been attracted by God *(ahl-e jazbeh)* must encounter a master to be guided from their own state of attraction to God to the state of social conduct on the Path *(soluk)*. To put it differently, they must be brought back to the state of sobriety *(sahv)* from their own state of drunkenness *(sokr)*, so that their drunkenness can be transformed back into a state of wakefulness.

There are, on the other hand, lovers and seekers of Truth who follow the path of *soluk* . Through love, service and struggling against self-worship, these people gradually traverse the Path. Most seekers of the Truth are in this state of *soluk,* although some travelers do reach the state of *soluk* from the station of divine attraction, and others reach the state of divine attraction while following the path of *soluk*—though the latter are brought back to the state of *soluk* through the aid of the guiding master.

It is important to note here that those who are attracted by God cannot reach perfection unless they enroll, as it were, in the school of the inward journey and social conduct. And those who are traveling on the path of inward journey and social conduct on the Path cannot reach perfection until they pass through the stage of divine attraction.

Thus, the seekers of God can be classified into four separate groups, namely: the attracted ones, the travelers, the attracted ones who later become travelers, and the travelers who later become attracted. However, out of these four groups, only the attracted ones who later become travelers are qualified to guide and lead others. The other three groups of people, though they may be very advanced Sufis, are not qualified to guide others. That is to say, only those Sufis who have first completed the stage of divine attraction and have then traveled the path of social conduct can be masters of the Path and as such guide others to God.

I hope that all lovers and seekers of the Truth will succeed in traveling the stages of love. I also would like to remind everyone that the main cornerstone of the building of *soluk* is service to humanity—regardless of color, race and creed—without expectation of anything in return.

A SELFLESS MASTER

Just as the more one knows about any given field of endeavor, the higher one rises in that field and the more respected one becomes, so on the Sufi Path the greater one's selflessness the more sublime and elevated one becomes.

Thus, the criterion for recognizing masters and *shaikhs* of the Path is their expression of nonexistence and their lack of pretension. The task of every master is to take away the traveler's ego and annihilate him in the ocean of God's Attributes and Essence. How can a self-absorbed master perform such a task?

The master of the Path is like a mirror reflecting the disciple's devotion to God and transmitting God's favor to the disciple. If the mirror of the heart of the master or *shaikh* bears the corrosion of being, a veil will fall between the Sufi and God so that instead of guiding and opening the way, the master or *shaikh* will block the Path for the traveler, turning the Sufi from the goal of God-worship to that of self-worship.

There are numerous examples of the selflessness of masters of the Path. Two particularly noteworthy ones are provided below:

It is recounted that when the Mongols invaded Iran one of them captured the well-known Sufi poet 'Attar with the intention of killing him. At this point, someone appeared, offering a thousand *dirhams* for him. 'Attar told the Mongol not to sell him, saying that the price was not right. Shortly after, as the Mongol was once again about to kill him, another buyer appeared. This time the offer was merely a sack of straw. 'Attar then exclaimed, "*Now* you can sell me, for that's my correct price!" Upon hearing this, the Mongol fell into a rage and cut off 'Attar's head.

One day, Abu Sa'id 'Abo'l-Khayr went to attend a memorial service, where he was met by the official presenters, who wanted to introduce him in the customary, elaborate way. They asked the master's disciples by what title they should announce him. Aware of what they were asking, the master told them, "Go and announce Nobody, the son of Nobody!" The presenters did accordingly. Hearing this, the eminent people assembled there looked up to find out who was coming. Seeing the master, they were overcome and burst into tears at his humility.

If individuals with the stature of 'Attar and Abu Sa'id did not dare to express self-existence, one must concede that the egotism and self-centeredness of the masters of today only demonstrate their own ignorance, arrogance and ambition.

SUBMISSION

Submission *(taslim)* means to give yourself to God unconditionally, wholeheartedly and without seeking anything in return. It means not allowing yourself to be disturbed by whatever God sends you, but rather always maintaining a cheerful countenance.

Only when the Sufi submits to God's will is he worthy of God's special attention and favor. The person who has not surrendered to God is like a nonconductive body that blocks the inflow of energy emanating from God's special mercy. When, however, the Sufi submits, he becomes a conductive body that receives endless blessings from the power of God's help.

Submission means eagerly and gladly welcoming whatever hardship and affliction God sends you, because it is His will. It means not questioning anything involving created beings, assuming that whatever seems wrong to you is due to your own ignorance, and being certain that no movement occurs in God's creation that is not in accordance with His will, that God is nothing but Absolute Goodness, and that whatever He does is good and right.

Submission to a master is the same as submission to God, for a master is God's representative on earth. The secret of submission to a master, in the beginning, is to practice the etiquette of submission so that ultimately you may truly submit to God. When you submit to a master, the master is obliged to instruct you in such a way that you may gradually come to submit to God, such that the self which stands between you and God disappears.

Once Jonaid was informed that Nuri had been standing in one place in his house for three days and nights, wailing without stopping. Jonaid went to see him and said, "If you are sure that this wailing is beneficial, then tell me why so that I may share in your knowledge. But if you do not believe that it is beneficial, then submit your heart, so that it may be glad." With this, Nuri stopped crying and exclaimed, "What a wise teacher Jonaid is!"

Those who have been slain
by the dagger of submission,
Every moment receive
new life from the Unseen.
The intellect cannot understand
the origin of this mystery,
For such slain ones
speak a different tongue.

—'Ayno'l-Qozat Hamadani

ETIQUETTE AND ETHICS

The etiquette and ethics of the Sufis reflect the way and custom of the highest, most perfected human beings. This etiquette and ethics involve a number of practices, the most important of which are as follows:

1. The Sufi gives precedence to all of creation over himself.
2. The Sufi is fair to all, yet expects fairness from no one.
3. The Sufi is kind and helpful to all, yet expects help and kindness from no one.
4. The Sufi is never self-centered or egocentric.
5. The Sufi serves all of God's creation.
6. The Sufi always observes the rights of others.
7. The Sufi loves all of God's creatures.
8. The Sufi praises all things created by God that are beautiful.
9. The Sufi harbors no resentment against anyone and regards no one as an enemy.
10. The Sufi takes the trouble to make things easy for others.
11. The Sufi never speaks with an acid tongue, always being kind and respectful toward others.
12. The Sufi is never pessimistic or depressed.
13. The Sufi never feels offended by anyone.
14. The Sufi neither complains about anyone nor claims anything for himself.

15. The Sufi is never mean or envious.

16. The Sufi never gets angry or harsh with anyone.

17. The Sufi keeps any promises he has made, even if his life must be sacrificed.

Those who consider themselves Sufis and do not possess this etiquette and ethics wear the Sufi garb under false pretenses and risk giving a bad name to those who are truly Sufis.

SIN AND MERIT

In addition to the conventional view of sin and merit in terms of the religious law, Sufism has a code of sin and merit of its own, a summary of which is provided below:

It is considered a sin for the novice Sufi to annoy or give trouble to anyone else; in fact, a Sufi should take care not to cause the slightest offense to others:

So long as you don't hurt others,
do what you will,
For in our religious law
there is no other sin but this.
—Hafez

As for the advanced Sufi, egocentricity is a sin. It has been said that one's being is a sin beyond compare with any other, and that a Sufi sins when his attention is on anything other than God.

Eliminate the sin
that is Maghrebi's existence;
Once that is done,
ask no more about sin.
—Maghrebi

For the novice Sufi, merit involves acquiring a heart and making others happy. As the saying goes: "If you walk on water, you're just a chip of wood *(khas)*; if you fly in the air, you're no more than a fly *(magas);* acquire a heart and become a true person *(kas).*"

It is related that Bayazid, on one of his trips to Mecca, came upon a well in the desert around which a crowd was gathered. Off to the side sat a dog, panting with thirst. Bayazid called out to the people, "Is there anyone among you who is willing to trade a little water for the merit of fifty years of fasting, prayer, pilgrimage and all my good works?" Someone who knew Bayazid said, "I'm willing!" The transaction was completed and the man gave Bayazid the water, which he, in turn, gave to the dog, giving his thanks to God.

The highest merit for the Sufi lies in not being conscious of the meritorious actions he performs, regarding them as insignificant. More importantly, the Sufis consider egocentricity and the assertion of existence, which derive from reason, to be sinful, while regarding the expression of the absence of self, or nonexistence, which is the product of divine love, as being worthy of merit.

The merit of fasting and valid pilgrimage
is earned by that person
Who has made the pilgrimage to the shrine
of the winehouse of love.

—Hafez

DETACHMENT FROM THE WORLD

Tajrid means severing oneself from attachments. This letting go of attachments does not imply being materially impoverished. A Sufi may have many possessions, but he is not attached to any of them.

Once Shah Nimatullah received a certain *darvish*, who stayed in his *khaniqah* for a few days. Noticing the splendor of the *khaniqah's* decor and furnishings, the Sufi thought in his heart that Sufism was incompatible with such worldliness and splendor. "What abundance one sees around here! It's more like a palace than a place of poverty!" the visitor thought to himself.

On the last day of his stay, he went to the master for permission to depart. Shah Nimatullah said, "O *darvish*, let me go with you." The Sufi exclaimed, "You are going to leave all this luxury and position and accompany a poor *darvish* like me?" Shah Nimatullah replied, "Of course! Why not?" And the two of them set out.

A few miles along the way, the *darvish* suddenly remembered that he had forgotten his *kashkul* (begging bowl) in the *khaniqah*. He turned to Shah Nimatullah and said in a worried tone, "I've left my *kashkul* behind! Why don't you sit down here and wait, while I run back and get it." Shah Nimatullah replied, "*Darvish*, I have left behind everything I had. Yet you cannot leave behind even a simple *kashkul*. You're not worthy of traveling with me." With this, he turned and left.

This is how Shah Nimatullah taught the *darvish* that outward poverty is no sign of detachment from the world. Rather, 'detachment from the world' *(tajrid)* means not being tied to the world or anything in it.

Whoever humbles himself in the dust
is elevated to liberation;
The seed planted deep in the earth
sprouts to rise above the soil.

Until you're detached from the world,
you cannot set out for the goal;
When the shell of the egg falls away,
then is the fledgling revealed.
—Anon.

THE MEANING OF *"YA 'ALI!"*

From time to time I have been asked why the Nimatullahi dervishes say, "*Ya 'Ali!*" Here is my reply:

Darvishes say, *"Ya 'Ali!"* to invoke the favor of the Name, *al-'Ali* ('the Sublime'), which is one of the Names of God.

It is from this Name, *al-'Ali,* that God's empowering strength emanates to the creation. To put it another way, the Name *al-'Ali* is the rope of God's empowering strength, which the *darvish* grips when finding himself entangled in social problems. Being helpless and incapable, the Sufi says, "There is no strength and no power but through God, the Sublime, the Magnificent."

Thus, Sufis in society say "*Ya 'Ali!*" as an appeal for help from God, as the 'Sublime', by taking refuge in His empowering strength from the calamities of the world.

In doing so, the Sufi is focused on God, not on any individual; his attention is directed towards God alone—and as such the Sufi is not a worshipper of an individual, but of God.

There is no one but God
in all the world;
Seek help from none
but Him.

UNBELIEF

The Sufis call feeling offended and consciousness of oneself unbelief *(kofr)*, which stems from dualism and idolatry.

It has been said that Islam consists of three degrees, the first being 'Islam' itself and the other two being 'faith' *(iman)* and 'beneficence' *(ehsan)*.

'Islam' is said to be when someone slaps you and you slap him back.

'Faith' is said to be when someone slaps you and you let it pass.

'Beneficence' is said to be when someone slaps you and not only do you not feel offended, but you display loving-kindness towards the person who slapped you.

The prime example of beneficence for Sufis from the early days of Islam is Malek-e Ashtar, a noted companion of the Prophet. One day, while in the marketplace, a man mistook him for a certain enemy and called him insulting names. After Malek had left, the merchants gathered around the man and asked if he knew the person to whom he had been speaking. The man replied, "Yes," and mentioned the name of his enemy. "You're wrong!" they exclaimed. "That was Malek-e Ashtar."

Shocked, the man ran after Malek to apologize. He found him in the mosque, saying his prayers. When his prayers were concluded, Malek stretched out his arms to offer a prayer of supplication on behalf of the man, saying, "O Lord, I entreat You not to punish that man for cursing me, for I was not offended. I hope You will forgive him."

If a Sufi feels offended, then he must be *someone,* whereas, in truth, a Sufi is no one, and one who is 'no one' cannot be offended by anyone.

We keep faith, accept all blame,
and are joyful,
For feeling offended
on our Path is unbelief.

On the Sufi Path, consciousness of oneself and self-satisfaction constitute 'unbelief', for a person who experiences such things worships both himself and God; he is dualist, not a Sufi. The Sufi believes in unity and nothing else. One who is conscious of God cannot be conscious of self.

Thought of oneself and self-satisfaction,
these do not exist in the world of the Sufi.
In our creed, such things
constitute unbelief.

THE PRISONERS OF THE *NAFS*

With great regret it must be conceded that certain masters of our time are themselves slaves to their *nafs*.

The *nafs* within them is so strong that it has commanded them to become Sufis for the purpose of becoming masters, so that they use this Path to fulfill their ambition and compensate for the setbacks in their lives.

Such 'masters' have used the *zekr* (remembrance of God), which is meant to be applied like an ax to the roots of their being, for the purpose of self-worship. They employ the remembrance of God as the capital for their own shops, solely to deceive people. The wine of divine love, which is meant to blind one to one's own existence, they pour down their front, mesmerized by the *nafs*, displaying it on the garment of hypocrisy and self-display, heedless of the fact that Sufism means the abandoning of outward pretension, not the claiming of spiritual guidance.

Furthermore, these 'masters' have faithful disciples, who, ruled by the *nafs*, perceive the fulfillment of the *nafs* in such 'masters'. As a result, these disciples, being unaware of the true nature of their so-called masters, submit to them so that their *nafs*-worship, like that of their masters, may be perfected.

As Rumi says:

Like to like
in this earth and heaven
Are drawn to one another
as iron to a magnet.

The remembrances that such 'masters' prescribe without authorization, being founded on the basis of the *nafs*, involve trickery and only serve to mislead the disciple, making him all the more a prisoner of the *nafs*.

What is even more remarkable is that the deceitful *nafs* can often produce visionary experiences and miraculous powers in the sleeping and waking states of these people. This, however, only serves to confirm their involvement in *nafs*-worship, since they are unaware that these are but tricks of the *nafs*. In this way, disciple and 'master' are kept contented and comfortable with each another. But alas, the Truth is missing between them! As Rumi describes it:

You're the disciple, the guest of one
Who, out of meanness, takes your gains.

He is not strong, so how can he make you strong?
He has no light; rather, he makes you dark.

Not having light himself, how can others
By associating with him gain light?

Like a blind man applying drugs to the eyes,
What can he put on your eyes other than wool?

There's no scent of God in him, not a trace;
Yet his claim is greater than that of Adam.

In his talk, he finds fault with Bayazid;
His inner being puts Yazid to shame.

He has stolen the words of the Sufis
So that others think he is someone special.

Even Satan is ashamed to show him his face
Since he claims he is higher than God's closest friends!

Destitute of bread or provisions from heaven,
He has not been thrown even a bone by God.

He has proclaimed, "I have laid out the feast!
I am God's chosen, the king's own son!

Welcome, simple-hearted ones, writhing in hunger;
At my festive table eat your fill—of nothing."

For years, on the promise of 'tomorrow', some people
Have gathered around that door; but 'tomorrow' never comes.

It takes a long time for a person's inner
Being to emerge in its entirety.

Once the seeker finds out that this 'master' is nothing,
His life has run out—So what good is this knowledge?

QUESTIONING

Once a seeker of the Path has found a master and submitted to him, he must not question the master's instruction, for a master knows secret things that the disciple is unable to perceive. Hence, if a master acts in a way that appears contrary to the disciple's nature, the latter should not question this, but rather have faith that the master knows better. By the same token, a disciple should not test the master, for this would undermine the disciple's devotional commitment, leading to his eventual break with the master. The traveler on the Path must be careful not to put himself unwittingly in danger of being cut off from the master's inward attention.

This matter is presented lucidly in the Koran through the story of Moses' encounter with Khezr, which may serve as a lesson illustrating the relationship between master and disciple:

One day Moses prayed to God, asking, "O Lord, is there any created being on earth who has greater knowledge than I?"

"O Moses," God replied, "I have a devotee named Khezr whose knowledge is greater than yours."

Moses then asked to be directed to him and was told by God that he could be found "between the two seas." Moses set out and found Khezr where God had indicated, whereupon Moses greeted him. Khezr responded by declaring, "Hail to you, O prophet of the Children of Israel!" Moses asked who had told Khezr that he was a prophet. The latter replied, "I was informed by the One who sent you to me."

Moses then explained he had come to Khezr to learn the knowledge that had been taught to him. "You cannot accompany me," said Khezr, "because you will not understand what I do and you do not have the capacity to accept it."

"If God wills," replied Moses, "you will find that I have the capacity to accept whatever you do."

Having warned Moses, Khezr went with him down to the sea, where they found a ship, which the captain let them board. No sooner were they on board than Khezr began to make a hole in the side of the ship, sinking it. Moses protested, "Why did you make a hole in the ship? People might have drowned! This truly is a strange thing!"

"Didn't I tell you that you would not have the capacity to accept what I do?" countered Khezr.

"I'm sorry!" pleaded Moses. "This is hard work. Be easy on me and give me another chance!"

Khezr agreed and they walked on until they came to a village by the sea. Impatient with hunger, Moses rushed off to ask the inhabitants for some food, but they refused him. On leaving the village, they came upon a wall that had collapsed. Khezr suddenly set to work building it up again. "They refuse us food," exclaimed Moses, "yet you rebuild their wall for them! You could at least have gotten paid for this work!"

"Now we must part ways!" declared Khezr "But first, I will explain my actions, which you did not have the capacity to accept. I put a hole in the ship because it belonged to some poor people and was their only means of livelihood. In that region there was a king who was seizing all ships. By putting a hole in it, I made it defective, so that the king wouldn't take it and thus the ship would remain in the hands of those poor people.

"As for the wall, it belonged to a pair of orphans, and under it was a treasure, which also belonged to them. God wanted to ensure that the treasure would eventually come into their hands, so I rebuilt the wall to protect it."

The moment Khezr finished speaking he disappeared, and Moses could never find him again.

As Rumi concludes:

Come into the protective shade of the sage
Whom no speaker can carry off from the way.

Seek to be near him in the way of God;
Never turn for a moment from your devotion to him.

Just as he may change a thorn to a rose,
He may bring light to an eye that is blind.

Initiate and devotee of one of God's elect,
The seeker may be borne by him to the presence of God.

When you choose your master, take care to submit;
Like Moses, proceed, commanded by Khezr.

Accept what Khezr does if you have no hypocrisy,
So he will not say, "This is the parting." (Koran XVIII: 78)

God has said the master's hand is as His own,
And declared, "The hand of God is above their hands."

When you've chosen your master, don't be fainthearted;
Don't be weak like water and crumbly like earth.

If every blow you receive makes you full of resentment,
How can you be a clear mirror, for the mirror must be
polished?

Annihilate your being in that of the Creator,
Like copper that melts in the alchemical fire.

MASTER AND DISCIPLE

The relationship between master and disciple is based on three principles:

1. The disciple's devotion *(eradat)* to a master,
2. The *zekr* that the master inculcates in the disciple, and
3. The master's attention (*nazar*) to the disciple.

1. The Disciple's Devotion to a Master

Every person wants to find a perfect human being with whom he may become harmonized in action, speech and thought. That is, all human beings, whether they know it or not, have their sights set on human perfection, desiring to find a teacher who may guide them towards it.

In seeking the way to perfection, a person may encounter a master and accept him with heart and soul as a guide and teacher. When one finds such a master, one devotes oneself to him in order to win his attention.

Devotion to a master can be compared to the crying of a baby for its mother's milk. When a baby cries out of hunger, its mother's milk is instinctively produced in the breast, which the mother places in the baby's mouth to suckle. The situation of the disciple with respect to a master is similar, where in expressing devotion the disciple naturally attracts the master's attention, so that the master may feed him the milk of spiritual cognitions and realities and quench his thirst in the quest for Reality.

As Rumi says:

The cloud must weep for the meadow to smile;
The child must cry for the milk to flow.

Devotion to a master also serves to draw the disciple from self-love to love of another; and self-love is a great obstacle to the perception of Reality. As the poet says:

Do not be like a dog, content with eating and sleeping;
Direct your love to another, even if only a cat.

Of course, the master here must be perfect to turn this love of another into the love of God, for if he is not perfect, a veil will descend between the disciple and God, and the disciple will fall prey to worship of an individual, which is itself but a form of self-worship.

2. Zekr

The following points must be made about the *zekr* that a master inculcates in his disciple:

First, through the *zekr* the disciple's attention gradually becomes directed away from consciousness of self to consciousness of God, turning him away from self-worship and attention to self. In the words of the poet:

I envisioned You so much that I became you entirely;
Little by little You approached, and bit by bit I went away.

Second, *zekr* helps to establish the spiritual relationship and bond with the master, enabling the disciple to generate and strengthen devotion to the master.

Third, through *zekr,* the disciple draws the inward attention of the master and attracts to the disciple the master's supportive aspiration *(hemmat).*

Fourth, through the link of *zekr*, the disciple eventually becomes one with the master, establishing a unity between them.

3. The Master's Attention to the Disciple

The master's spiritual attention *(nazar)* is the foundation of the Path. As noted above, the disciple's devotion and persistence in *zekr* serves to draw the attention of the master, which, in turn, brings God's favor to the disciple. As the poet says:

Forty retreats, forty retreats, O forty retreats!
One glance of attention from the master
is worth a hundred retreats.

If the attention of a perfect master does not accompany the *zekr* when it is being inculcated, the *zekr* will bear no fruit. The master's attention in the *zekr* is so important that any word accompanied by the master's attention while being inculcated in the disciple will in fact be effective in purifying the disciple—even if such a word is not a name of God.

The following story illustrates this point:

When Moshtaq 'Ali Shah Esfahani was staying in Kerman, he was the object of the jealousy of the exoteric clergy, who paid a prostitute to try to seduce him. She went to Moshtaq and began flirting with him in the hope of leading him astray. The more Moshtaq exercised forbearance, the more persistent the woman became, until finally he ordered, "Get out, you whore!" Since Moshtaq accompanied these words with his spiritual attention for the purpose of reforming her state, they affected her heart. As she went home, the words, "Get out, you whore!" became her *zekr*. Repeating them over and over, she abandoned prostitution and eventually became a friend of God *(wali)*.

RIGHT AND WRONG

In addition to their traditional religious meanings, the terms 'practicing right' *(amr-e be ma'ruf)* and 'forbearing from wrong' *(nahy-e az monkar)* also have another meaning in Sufism.

In Sufi terminology, 'right' means serving God, and 'wrong' means associating with the *nafs*; put another way, 'right' is God, and 'wrong' is the creation.

By practicing right and forbearing from wrong, the Sufis mean that people should get away from egotism and become closer to God.

When Bayazid was asked about practicing right and forbearing from wrong, he explained, "Try to be in a region where right and wrong do not exist, for both exist in the region of the creation. On the plane of unity, there is neither 'practicing right' nor 'forbearing from wrong'."

In both worlds, only God is 'right';
The only 'wrong' in being is the ego.

'Wrong' appears as the face of multiplicity;
That which is 'right' is pure unity.

Put being away; pass 'wrong' by,
So that 'right' may appear before your eyes.

As long as you are absorbed in self,
know that you are 'wrong'.
Let yourself go and be freed from duality.

The only 'wrong' in existence is you;
The appearance of you has separated you from Existence.

For the Sufi, what is other than God is 'wrong';
Hence, he flees from what is other than God.

Because 'right' can mean nothing but unity,
The Sufi directs himself towards that unity.

On this Path there is no 'wrong' but you,
And there is no 'right' but God.

SPIRITUAL COMBAT

The Prophet once said, "We have returned from the lesser spiritual combat to the greater." Upon hearing this, his followers asked, "O Prophet of God, what is the greater spiritual combat?" He replied, "Struggle with the *nafs*."

Indeed, to attain God one must wage spiritual combat *(jehad)* with the *nafs*, and Sufis devote most of their time to this combat with the *nafs*. Of the thousands who embark on the Path and engage in such combat, only a few are successful, for the *nafs* is so cunning that whenever it is chased out one door, it comes back in through another. At times, it may tell you to practice strict discipline; it may command you to undergo long and harsh asceticism. At other times, it may urge you to be a master, telling you that you are a perfect human being and that it is your duty to guide others. It may even go so far as to say that you are higher than Bayazid or Jonaid and that no one is higher than you in adhering to divine unity *(tawhid)*.

As Rumi says:

> *If the* nafs *tells you to fast and pray,*
> *It's but a trickster, hatching a plot against you.*

The only way one may come to recognize the *nafs'* magic spells is through the guidance of a master who is aware of the heart, and spiritual combat can be waged only through the power of love and devotion to such a master.

In Sa'di's words:

> *To me, you are not one who breaks the unbeliever;*
> *If you are a man, break the unbelieving* nafs.

DR. JAVAD NURBAKHSH

THE FAMILY

With the number of Sufis steadily increasing and with growing numbers of them showing perceptible progress, I find it necessary to point out that it is quality, not quantity, that matters on the Path, and that it is the spiritual state of Sufis that counts, not their number.

In light of this, I feel compelled to speak of the family of Sufis, for those who come from all over the world to join this Path all become members of the family of Sufis. The sense of belonging one gains when one joins this Sufi family is based on love, kindness and loyalty. All are brothers and sisters here without distinction, regardless of sex, race, material circumstances or education. All have the same common goal of human perfection.

There are, of course, conditions for entering the Sufi family and being allowed to sit in the circle of the Sufis. All who have joined this family know and have accepted these conditions, undertaking to observe all of them. Unfortunately, however, within a few months of joining, by not living up to their undertaking, most people find themselves, without realizing it, outside the family, or circle, of Sufis. To tell the truth, among the *darvishes* who gather in each *khaniqah* there are really very few actual Sufis. The majority are no more than spectators from outside the Sufi family, even though they may be physically seated in the assembly.

A simple example may serve to illustrate this point: An egg may be transformed into a chick by the mother hen sitting on it. However, if the egg remains for a time outside the protective nest that the hen provides, it has no chance of becoming a chick; and what is more, it is, alas, no longer even a viable egg.

In the realm of Sufism, the same thing is true. In agreeing to all the conditions of initiation and undertaking to observe the fundamental vows, a Sufi takes the first step on the Path in the hope of becoming transformed in that favorable environment, gradually traversing the stages to perfection. But, if for some reason he ceases to fulfill his obligations and consciously or unwittingly leaves the circle, thus forfeiting the opportunity of being a true lover of God, nothing can be done. Such a person can never reach perfection, and no amount of time or effort will have any effect.

In this context, I see many people who sit in the circle of Sufis and yet are alien to Sufism. I keep silent about the presence of such people, saying nothing, because I believe that a spectator may take part, may sit in any gathering without any harm being done. Yet I feel sorry for these people, for they are only deceiving themselves.

KHANIQAH AND RELIGIOUS ASSEMBLIES

The *khaniqah* is a place for a particular group of persons, not just anyone, and as such it possesses certain standards and aims that distinguish it from other religious assemblies.

Most people go to religious assemblies to learn not to offend others, whereas the Sufi goes to the *khaniqah* to learn not to feel offended by others.

Most people turn to religious assemblies to ensure that their lives in the world are secure and that their afterlives are taken care of. The Sufi turns to the *khaniqah* to forget the world and the hereafter and to embrace the eternal Beloved.

Most people go to religious assemblies to attain heaven. The Sufi goes to the *khaniqah* to seek refuge in God from the self.

Most people go to religious centers to rid themselves of bad qualities. The Sufi goes to the *khaniqah* to wipe away the pattern of existence with the help of love and intoxication.

Most people go to religious assemblies to pray for the stability of their religion and their lives. The Sufi goes to the *khaniqah* to silence his claim to existence and to become consumed in the fire of divine love.

Most people go to religious centers to improve their condition, to make it better for themselves. The Sufi goes to the *khaniqah* to forget the self, to *not* be himself.

GOD'S BENEVOLENCE AND WRATH

Benevolence *(lotf)* and wrath *(qahr)* are both qualities of God. The Sufi who is truly in love with God loves both of these Attributes equally. Rumi writes:

I am in love with both
His benevolence and wrath:
How amazing that I should love
these two opposites.

Due to the manifestation of divine benevolence and wrath, the Sufi will encounter many tests on the Path by which he will have the opportunity to demonstrate the degree of his sincerity, devotion and submission to God. The Sufi thus accepts divine wrath, as well as benevolence, wholeheartedly. Not only does the Sufi not become worried or upset in encountering divine wrath, he even rejoices in it, knowing that whatever comes from the Beloved is pleasant and good.

In one of the stories about the famous lovers Layla and Majnun, it is related that Layla was one day preparing a meal for the people in her neighborhood. Like everyone else, Majnun took a bowl and went to her house to partake in the festivities and eat. When the time for the meal came, Layla herself served everyone the food. As Majnun approached her, however, she grabbed his bowl and smashed it to the ground, breaking it to pieces.

Later, Majnun was asked by the people at the gathering about Layla's strange behavior and why she had treated them so much better than him. In answer, he replied:

If she really desired any of you,
why then did she break only my bowl?

In this same context, a great Sufi has written:

Sorrow and pain both come from the Friend;
How pleasing it is that He should remind me
To remember Him through this sorrow and pain.

SELFLESSNESS

The *khaniqah* is the school of nonexistence and selflessness. Therefore, the *shaikh* of the *khaniqah* must strive more than anyone for nonexistence, and his service must be greater than anyone else's in order to encourage novice Sufis and others connected to the *khaniqah* in the enthusiastic pursuit of their spiritual duties.

Being in charge of a *khaniqah* is a position that demands selflessness. If the *shaikh* or the person who is in charge of a *khaniqah* does not manifest such a state, he has demonstrated his unworthiness to hold this position.

The person in charge of the *khaniqah* must not give orders harshly. If he wants someone to do something, he must present the matter with the utmost humility. If the person in charge of the *khaniqah* is authoritarian or status-seeking, novice Sufis will be frightened away and even Sufis of long-standing will eventually be driven to leave.

The *shaikh* of the *khaniqah* is like a parent to the Sufis, although a parent without personal expectations or motives. And children who experience unkindness from their parents often run away from home.

I am stressing this point to emphasize that Sufis' willingness or unwillingness to come to the *khaniqah* is ultimately the responsibility of the person who is in charge of the *khaniqah*, and this person should not blame others for a lack of enthusiasm in coming to the *khaniqah*.

To conclude, Sufis must be aware that in our eyes the most selfless person is the truest Sufi. A Sufi who is authoritarian and domineering is still but a prisoner of the unbelieving *nafs*.

BREATH IS THE TRUTH

Sufis have an expression, "breath is the truth". Beginners on the Path should know that the breath or word of the master, *shaikh*, and the advanced on the Path is an expression of the truth and therefore should be followed with contentment. When a Sufi does not carry out the orders of the master or *shaikh*, it is said that he has "killed" the breath of the master or the *shaikh*.

As for the perfected and heart-possessing Sufis, whatever they might hear, be it words from people or sounds around them, they should consider it as being primarily addressed to them so that they might learn something about their own progress and conduct on the Path.

It is related that Shibli was once in a market place when he heard a gypsy calling out "*S'tara barri*", which was a fragrant plant used as a spice in food.

Upon hearing the gypsy's words, Shibli fell down unconscious. When he regained consciousness, he was asked what had happened. In response he said, "Did you not hear God say: "*S'tara berri*" (which means 'strive to see My Goodness')?"

Sufis must listen with their hearts to the words of the *shaikhs* and the advanced in the *khaniqah*, follow their orders without question, and consider these 'breaths' as coming from God. The least that one might receive from such actions is this: by not insisting upon one's own point of view and thought, the traveler will be saved from being opinionated and self-centered.

As Hafez says:

In the world of the Sufis,
there is no thought and opinion stemming from the self.

In this religion, to see oneself and be opinionated
is but infidelity.
Although union with Him cannot be attained
through one's efforts,
strive, O heart, as much as you can.

FREEWILL AND DETERMINISM

If, in the beginning of the Path, the traveler believes in determinism, he will be an unbeliever. On the other hand, if, after completing the Path, such a traveler believes in his own freewill, then he will also be an unbeliever.

The point here is this: In the beginning of the Path, Sufis should depend solely upon their own efforts and should not consider states to be determined in any way.

There is a Persian proverb that says: "Not everyone who runs after a gazelle catches it, but the one who catches the gazelle must first have run after it." In the beginning of the Path, travelers must believe in their own freewill. Gradually, as travelers advance on the Path, their own freewill diminishes and God's control over them increases in such a way that at the end of the Path, after the army of desire and passion has been defeated and the army of love has conquered the city of the heart, the transitory self will become annihilated in the Absolute Being. If at this stage travelers still believe in their own freewill, then they are unbelievers, for real Sufis at this stage are so annihilated in God that they completely become Him. Therefore, such Sufis do not have any ego to enable them to have wishes, and they do not have any desires by which to choose. At this point, they have reached the stage of submission and contentment, and together with the poet say:

The Friend has fastened a rope around my neck
and drags me wherever He desires.

WHO IS A SUFI?

Many of us proudly call ourselves Sufis without truly understanding what Sufism is or who the Sufis are. Day and night, we engage in idolatry and pursue the desires of the *nafs*. This situation is summed up in Rumi's verse:

The Sufis are disgraced because of our behavior,
our constant concern with our own desires.

In the traditional practice of Sufism, which is based on the Islamic principle of adherence to divine unity (*tawhid),* only someone who is truly without self, without existence, who has no concern for the material world and whose attention is focused solely and entirely on the divine Beloved is worthy of the name 'Sufi'.

Khwaja 'Abdo'llah Ansari has described the Sufis as "a group who are never entangled in the thicket of envy, whose robes of submission are never tainted with the dust of the *nafs*, and whose eyes are never bothered by the smoke of selfish desire. They are monarchs of the Path in the garb of poverty, and angelic in their human form, while proceeding in a stately manner along their way."

With this description in mind, it would be well for us to sit in judgment upon our claim to be Sufis, analyzing it critically, determining just how much of a 'Sufi' we are, with the aim of trying to correct whatever deficiency keeps us from fully becoming a Sufi.

The first lesson of Sufism is to love God's creatures and respect their views. Therefore, a Sufi should, in principle, refrain from interfering in others' affairs or condemning their way of thinking. Anyone who condemns other people's religious convictions or manner of worship—which are ways of attracting God's favor and moving closer to

Him—not only is not a Sufi, but is, in fact, an enemy of the Sufis, for objecting to others' religious views in any way is a form of arrogance and self-centeredness, constituting the greatest offense in Sufism.

Together, we must free Sufism from dogmatism and pretension and work at protecting the basis of Sufi spirituality from hypocrisy. We should be especially mindful of the fact that Sufism is the school of humanity. Without emphasis on inward spirituality and purity, one cannot, properly speaking, develop into a true human being, truly love all humanity, or serve others with heart and soul without any thought of reward.

THE INTELLECT

The question often arises of what the role of the intellect is in Sufism. To begin with, let us identify three categories of people in this context: first, the ordinary; second, scholars and intellectuals; and third, the Sufis.

The ordinary are those who are ruled by the *nafs* and governed by the intellect only from time to time.

As for scholars and intellectuals, they live by the lamp of the intellect in such a way that their *nafs* fulfills its desires with the aid of the intellect. Of course, the *nafs* occasionally embarrasses them by ignoring the intellect and pursuing its own inclinations.

The root meaning of the Arabic word for 'intellect' *('aql)* is 'to hobble a steed.' Thus, one may say that the intellect 'hobbles' that drunken camel which constitutes one's selfish desires, keeping the *nafs* from running rampant and doing whatever it wishes. Sometimes, however, this drunken camel breaks the hobble and bolts, creating catastrophe all around.

The Sufis are those whose intellect is sincerely obedient to love. In the early stages of the Path, the *nafs* may in fact be in league with the intellect to lead the Sufi astray, but in the final stages, once the army of love has completely defeated the inclinations of the *nafs*, the intellect becomes the sincerely devoted servant of the Sufi.

Dr. Javad Nurbakhsh

THE BENEFITS OF GOING TO THE *KHANIQAH*

Sufis benefit from going to the *khaniqah* in four ways: First of all, human beings are forgetful by nature and therefore need constant reminding. The purpose of going to the *khaniqah* is to help Sufis remain conscious of their vow to God and to keep them aware so as not to forget God for even the blink of an eye. As Hafez writes:

Do not forget the King—
even for an instant;
For He might just look at you then,
and you will not even notice.

Going to the *khaniqah* reinforces this point in the Sufi's heart, for in the early stages of the Path one's *nafs* seeks to turn one away from God. One of the methods or tricks of the *nafs* is to persuade the Sufi that regular attendance at the *khaniqah* is not necessary, saying, "There's no point in it for you!" The *nafs* uses countless devices such as this to prevent the Sufi from going to the *khaniqah*, for when the *nafs* separates one from the community of Sufis, one is more easily distracted by one's own desires. As a consequence, one eventually ceases to remember God at all.

The second benefit of attending the *khaniqah* sessions is indicated in the Sacred Tradition: "I sit with the one who remembers Me." That is, the assembly of Sufis is the site of God's manifestation. The Sufi who joins the other Sufis in the *khaniqah* sits before God. This serves to aid the Sufi in becoming separated from the self, in coming to know and be associated with the realm of unity. For this reason, sitting in the circle of the Sufis is especially crucial in the early stages, in order to refine the heart and purify the inward being. The novice Sufi who spends a few hours a week at the *khaniqah* remembering God and forgetting the self is aided considerably in the journey to God. In fact, this allows him to practice nonexistence before the Existence of the Absolute. Furthermore, it serves to keep the Sufi attentive to God from one meeting to the next.

The third benefit of going to the *khaniqah* is that when several hearts are gathered together to remember God, they receive more help and blessings from God. This divine attention may have a powerful effect on the purification of the novice and can speed his advancement on the Path.

Finally, observing the conduct, speech and states of advanced Sufis in the *khaniqah* has a profound effect on the outward and inward being of the novice Sufi, inspiring him to strive to attain the spiritual states of those who are more experienced, helping him still further in progressing on the spiritual journey.

DEVOTION

Sufism is the school of divine ethics, and the master of the Path attempts to decorate the Sufi's heart with divine attributes.

In truth, the master of the Path is like an alchemist who transmutes the traveler's copper-like heart into gold through the alchemy of his attention and teaching. The fire needed to smelt the copper of the heart, and thereby transmute it into gold through the master's alchemy, is called devotion *(eradat).* Without the fire of devotion, the copper of the heart will not burn, nor will the master's alchemy take effect:

Humans and angels all exist
because of love;
Show your devotion so that you may reap
the blessings of this love.

The more scorching the fire of this devotion is, the sooner the master's alchemy will take effect. This is why the great Sufis have always emphasized that unless one purifies one's devotion towards the master, thereby drawing his attention, even years of asceticism and spiritual struggle will lead nowhere.

Know then that you should surrender to a perfect master with your heart and soul so that the master, through the alchemy of his attention, will be able to transmute your copper-like heart into gold, decorating your heart with divine attributes and ethics. Only in this way will your self finally be taken away, such that only He remains.

RULES AND MANNERS

The Sufi's attention must be directed solely towards God in the *khaniqah,* and he should not be concerned with anyone or anything else. It is related that Bayazid served Imam Jafar Sadeq as his disciple for six years. One day Imam Jafar asked him to fetch a book from the shelf. "What shelf?" Bayazid asked. "You have been coming here for six years and still don't know where the bookshelf is?" Imam Jafar asked in astonishment. Bayazid replied, "I come here for God's sake, not for the sake of anything else."

Sufis should be silent in the *khaniqah,* for by talking they may divert other people's attention from God to themselves. If they must talk, they should not speak loudly, for this too may distract other people's concentration on God. For the same reason, while drinking tea or eating, they should avoid being noisy with cup or plate.

During the sessions, Sufis should not lean against the wall or anything else, for just as Sufis do not inwardly rely upon anything other than God, so outwardly they should behave in a similar manner.

In short, if after leaving the *khaniqah* a Sufi were to be asked about the people or the things that he had seen in the *khaniqah,* the Sufi should be able to say that he does not remember seeing anyone or anything. Such is the way and manner of the sincere travelers on the Path, who are concerned solely with liberating themselves from the world of multiplicity and entering the world of unity, this being the true goal of humanity.

APHORISMS

O Sufi!

The basis of Sufism is consideration of the hearts and feelings of others. If you haven't the will to gladden someone's heart, then at least beware lest you hurt someone's heart, "for on our Path no sin exists but this."

O Sufi!

Since everything is one and the One is everything, try to love and serve all, so that you will be able to love the One (the Truth).

O Sufi!

There are two types of people. The behavior and thoughts of the first type are constructive while those of the second type are destructive. Try to assist the first group through love and encouragement and to guide the second group through friendship and understanding.

O Sufi!

The Supreme Name of God reveals the true inner being of a Sufi. Thus, if you see a Sufi who is a demon, that person was but a demon masquerading as a Sufi—fault is not to be found with Sufism.

The Name Supreme shall do its work:
do not worry O heart;
dissimulation and deceit can't change
a demon into Solomon.

—Hafez

O Sufi!

If you step upon love's ground with any sense of 'me' and 'thee' or self-identity, ultimately you will find yourself in the company of Eblis and Pharaoh, with no other gain but pretension, remorse and anxiety.

If, however, devoid of the conceit of 'me' and 'thee' and self-identity, you make your way with nothingness and self-negation through love's precincts, ultimately you will attain Divine Unity and Oneness and pluck the fruit of the tree of contentment, submission and tranquillity.

Therefore, take care to take the first step properly!

O Sufi!

Sincerity is the sign of psychological health. Sincerity means that whatever you show yourself as is what you really are, so that your outer being and your inner being become one. This is the real beginning of Sufism.

O Sufi!

The Sufi's only real miracle is non-being. To claim miraculous powers is to express 'being', and on the Path this is unbelief. The master of the Path is an idol-breaker, not an idol-maker. With this in mind, be sure to distinguish between commercial Sufism and true Sufism, so that you will recognize the false pretenders who only set traps.

O Sufi!

Drug addiction debases the character of human beings. Do not trust those who are addicted, for they break their promises easily and are contemptuous of human values. Thus, if you are a person of feeling, beware of addiction, for it will gradually destroy your constancy, stability and fidelity.

O Sufi!

What is Sufism?

Sufism is the apprehension of Reality through the attraction of divine love. It is the struggle to bring about unity of attention in both one's inner and outer being, under the guidance of a master of the Path. In other words, Sufism means looking in one direction and seeing all things as One.

O Sufi!

Fortune-telling, divination, occult practices and the like are the occupations of people who are charlatans and parasites, who are not productively occupied. Those who are interested in superstitious things are people of weak character, who take from others as a way of life.

There is no place in the world of Sufism for this kind of deceit and trickery. Beware, do not let yourself be fooled by these deceitful individuals.

O Sufi!

Sufism is based on chivalry, which is composed of selfless service and acknowledgment of the rights of others.

Strive to honor the pledge that you have made to God and to the master of the Path, for a person's worth lies in the fidelity of this pledge. Unfaithful and unreliable people have no access to love and purity.

O Sufi!

When you do a kindness for someone, forget about it; when someone does you a kindness, however, always keep it in mind. Ingratitude and neglect of the master's teaching are not only unworthy of a Sufi, but an ungrateful person is not even fit to be considered a human being. Indeed, such a person is lower than an animal.

O Sufi!

Most depression and agitation arise from material problems and emotional frustration. A Sufi, however, desires nothing but God and therefore is always content.

If there is any profit in this worldly market,
it is with the contented Sufi—
Lord, bestow on me the blessing of Sufism
and contentment!

—Hafez

O Sufi!

Sufis must in every respect endure whatever troubles may be imposed upon them by their fellow Sufis or others, accepting such troubles wholeheartedly. At the same time, they must under no circumstances inflict their own problems on others. To put it another way, Sufis must bear the burdens of others, but not impose any burdens upon them. They should be kind and loving towards everyone without expecting kindness or love in return.

O Sufi!

Sufism is the school of liberation, and the *khaniqah* is the place of the truly liberated. Beware that you do not tell others what to do or impose your views on others, for each heart has its own kind of connection with God, and any such connection is worthy of the Sufi's respect.

O Sufi!

Sufis are expected to be honest, to keep their promises and to be chivalrous on all occasions. In your interactions with others, therefore, behave in such a manner that you do not cause them to lose hope in humane behavior. If people become disappointed by you, they may be turned away from such humane behavior themselves. In this case, you will have so disgraced the school of love and purity that you will never be able to make amends.

O Sufi!

Since the basic principle of the Nimatullahi Sufi Order is the education, training and reform of society, anyone who seeks to gain entrance into the circle of the Sufis is admitted here. If a person takes even one step forward on this Path and is successful in self-purification, this in itself is of service to humanity. In light of this, occasionally persons may be found among the Sufis whose behavior does not match the conduct expected of Sufis, who on occasion do things that are quite improper. If you run across such a person, do not be antagonized and wonder, "What sort of Sufi is this?" Rather, consider what this person would be doing if he were not a Sufi!

O Sufi!

Be aware that the *khaniqah* is the place of fearless qalandars (those who put God before everything else), not of impure individuals devoted to indulging their passions. It is the haven of rends (those who are liberated from the affairs of the world, who have offered themselves up to God), not a place for prisoners of the world of dust and clay.

Here, there is no talk of 'I' and 'you'; all talk is of 'He' *(Hu)* and is for His sake. Though Sufis may appear to number in the thousands, they are in essence but One.

This is the place of non-being, not of 'I am this' and 'You are that'. If you are attached to 'who you are', then do not bother to enter here. But if you are a friend of God and unaware of yourself, then you will be welcome to sit in the humble circle of the Sufis.

O Sufi!

The Sufi is the partisan of union, not disunion. When you create a bond of love with someone, do not break it for it is not the way of the Sufi to break such a bond: this is infidelity in the creed of lovers.

If you do not want your Beloved to break the bond of love with you, take care not to break the bond of your affection with others; nor should you turn away from those who have turned away from you.

Preserve the love of others, so that God may preserve your own.

O Sufi!

Sufism is a Path leading one from the self to the heart and ending in the realm of unity. The traversing of this Path is possible only with the feet of nonexistence, the power of sincerity and the aid of love. Only when you are ready to travel selflessly and with sincerity will the force of love, which is God's favor, assist you in your journey.

Beware! This Path is not within the capacity of ordinary people: it is the way of the elect. If you do not truly give up your self, you will never reach the world of unity and detachment.

O Sufi!

No one ever became a Sufi simply by claiming to know the fundamental principles of Sufism. A Sufi is something to become, not something to read or hear about.

Bring acts, not mere claims!
For no safer path
Exists for the friends of God
than the way of tracelessness.

—Sa'di

O Sufi!

Your value is measured by your readiness to honor your pledges. It is the way of the Sufis to keep their word and never break it.

Try to keep the pledge to which you have committed yourself, for you can be sure that those who break their promises have no possibility of advancing on the Path. Furthermore, if you commit yourself to one who breaks his promises, you risk being betrayed, for those who break their promises all too easily abandon their commitments when their own interests are at stake.

O Sufi!

Where there is talk of 'I and you' and miraculous powers, Sufism does not exist. Where pretension and self-existence are expressed, Truth does not exist. The criterion of being a Sufi is selflessness. The more selfless you are, the more a Sufi you become.

O Sufi!

Sufism is not a matter of the clothes one wears. A Sufi should dress so as not to attract attention to himself, for the people of God reside in the place of the heart, not the material world. Rather than being concerned with the outward, strive in divine love to purify your heart of everything other than the Beloved.

O Sufi!

To serve God's creatures is to serve God. If you love God, then serve His creatures. Be aware that on this Path to make someone happy is a thousand times better than to indulge oneself, day and night, in prayers and invocations.

O Sufi!

Disturbing any aspect of God's creation only disturbs one's conscience and psychological health. This is why an aggressor always loses, no matter what the cause. Take care, therefore, not to disturb others.

O Sufi!

Be loving towards all God's creatures and appreciate whatever kindness they show you. At the same time, overlook their flaws, for in this way you will enjoy a spiritual heaven in this world.

O Sufi!

The basis of Sufism is the observance of etiquette, and the etiquette of Sufism lies in nonexistence. Therefore, it is impertinent and self-indulgent to be talkative, just as it is offensive to stare at an advanced one on the Path, for all of these things express existence.

O Sufi!

Observe the demands of friendship and never forget people's kindness to you. To take advantage of someone's hospitality—that is, to go to someone's home, eat his food, yet afterwards criticize him—is the practice of lowly, selfish individuals.

Should you encounter such a person who claims to be a Sufi, be aware that he has not understood anything about Sufism and has not taken even one step on the path of loving-kindness.

O Sufi!

Leave this world to the people of the world and the hereafter to the people of the hereafter. Submit the hand of devotion to God and place His love, which is the alchemy of eternal blessing, in the treasury of your heart, casting whatever is other than God into the crucible of oblivion.

Nimatullahi Sufi Order

Centers in North America, Western Europe, Australia and Africa

306 West 11th Street
New York, New York 10014
U.S.A.
Tel: 212-924-7739

4931 MacArthur Blvd. NW
Washington, D.C. 20007
U.S.A.
Tel: 202-338-4757

84 Pembroke Street
Boston, Massachusetts 02118
U.S.A.
Tel: 617-536-0076

4021 19th Avenue
San Francisco, California 94132
U.S.A.
Tel: 415-586-1313

11019 Arleta Avenue
Mission Hills, Los Angeles,
California 91345, U.S.A.
Tel: 818-365-2226

219 Chace Street
Santa Cruz, California 95060
U.S.A.
Tel: 408-425-8454

310 NE 57th Street
Seattle, Washington 98105
U.S.A.
Tel: 206-527-5018

4642 North Hermitage
Chicago, Illinois 60640
U.S.A.
Tel: 312-561-1616

405 Greg Avenue
Santa Fe, New Mexico 87501
U.S.A.
Tel: 505-983-8500

41 Chepstow Place
London W2 4TS,
England
Tel: 171-229-0769

95 Old Lansdowne Road
West Didsbury, Manchester
M20 8NZ, England
Tel: 161-434-8857

Kölnerstraße 176
51149 Köln
Germany
Tel: 2203-15390

50 rue du Quatrième Zouaves
Rosny-sous-Bois 93110,
Paris, France
Tel: 48552809

C/Abedul 11
Madrid 28036
Spain
Tel: 350-2086

87A Mullens St.
Balmain 2041,
Sydney, Australia
Tel: 555-7546

63 Boulevard Latrille
BP 1224 Abidjan,
CIDEX 1 Côte d'Ivoire, Africa
Tel: 410510

Quartier Beaurivage
BP 1599 Porto-Novo
Bénin
Tel: 214194

1784 Lawrence Avenue West
North York, Toronto, Ontario
Canada M6L 1E2
Tel: 416-242-9397

116 avenue Charles de Gaulle
69160 Tassin-La-Demi-Lune
France
Tel: 78342016